Island
of Tears

WILLIAM RONALD HAWKINS

Island of Tears

EFSTATHIADIS GROUP

EFSTATHIADIS GROUP S.A.
14, Valtetsiou Str.
106 80 Athens
Tel: (01) 5254650, 6450113
Fax: (01) 5254657
GREECE

ISBN 960 226 301 6

© **Efstathiadis Group S.A. 1998**

Captions accompanying pictures of the Island are extracts
from the poem "Spinaloga" by William Ronald Hawkins.

Island of tears: paintings by Michael Scarp
for the island of Spinaloga

Printed and bound in Greece

"A son's last thought should be for his mother ... A mother's last thought should be with her son."

Island of tears
by
William Ronald Hawkins

This epic poem of some seven hundred lines is written in English. It tells the tragic story of a Cretan youth, whom having caught lepracy, leaves his family in Crete to live on the Island of Spinalonga.

Having come to terms with his illness, he meets and marries Alis, and together they have a son. When he learns that the son is 'not a leper', and will be taken from him, he asks his wife to condone the exchange of leper blood. This she does with great reluctance, and some weeks later, full of the guilt, she takes her life. The child Roberto having reached the age of seven is to be visited by an old family friend, who having himself been cured from the disease comes to the Island to take Roberto and his father to the mainland. The child tragically dies during sleep, leaving the father with no alternative other than to come to terms with his God, and the entire poem takes the form of his suicide note.

Preface

The epic poem 'Island of tears'
which is purely fictional traces
the life of a leper who has to come
to terms with his illness, his life
and his God.

It is a study of the very close
relationship between a father and his
son, and a man's desperation to keep
such a relationship intact.

Written with intense feeling and passion,
the writer transmits the anxiety and
selfishness of a man hopelessly perplexed
by the conditions of his life.

The intenseness of the subject is
never better emphasised than in the
deliberately mis-rythmed verse
"and in my heart I hurt", where by
substituting the word hurt for bled
the poet cleverly emphasises the
subject's state of mind.

Whether or not you can sympathise
with the subject, you will want
to read this poem over and over again
and not be afraid to cry!

"My father had drawn a circle
for his family a ring"

Island of tears

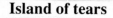

Perhaps I was a bit naive
perhaps I should have known
but the day I first met Basil
he was lying all alone
lying in a bed of clay
a youth all skin and bone

He'd come amongst a gang of thugs
and they in their play
had left the boy almost dead
in such a bad way
a letter 'L' on a broken bell
was carved in blood and clay

they'd took from him his ragged coat
and threw such heavy stones
that lay him so badly cut
that I could see his bones
I bandaged him as well as I could
despite his hurtful groans

I'd wanted to take him home that day
to take the cripple by the hand
to show to him my family
that he might understand
the meaning of love and friendship
within a family band

I knew papa would not approve
so I held his hand awhile
until he finally bade me leave
and with a youthful smile
he tried to lift and wave an arm
but his wounds they looked so vile

13

a curious knell sounded in that bell
as I awoke from dream

My father had drawn a circle
for his family a ring
and none of us must leave it
or take another in
our bonding would be binding
and protect us from within

Mother had died when we were young
so a mother I'd never seen
but I had a twin sister Stella
we were both now fourteen
and she was as good as a mother
if anyone could have been

My father worked so very hard
to keep that ring intact
he had such rigid values
that sometimes it was hard to act
in a manner he found pleasing
though in heart he nothing lacked

In his heart he loved his children
and expressed the point of view
that a man should live for his children
and this he made sure I knew
experience would tell only too well
whether such a sentiment was true

Several years had gone by
when I first felt the strain
it seemed to come and quickly go
but my energy would drain
and then one day my skin split
and with it came enormous pain

sparks fly in the sky
an angry Thor above

When papa first saw the cut
he viewed it with alarm
"It looks such an unfriendly wound
that gapes upon your arm
you must let me dress it son
or the wound will cause you harm"

He nursed my arm for many days
it looked so dreadfully unholy
and took such a deal from me
that soon I felt quite poorly
papa called the doctor
and the light faded slowly

"My boy a leper" I heard him say
"my boy so good and kind
he never did a bad thing
and yet it seems I find
that God has done this to him
and God is so unkind"

"Tell me doctor what can be done
why does he look so pale
will rest not cure him
all other treatments fail
will everything we do doctor
all be to no avail?"

the doctor slowly shook his head
and paced the wooden floor
"I do not have a treatment
and I fear still more
this broken skin will worsen
and his arm I'll have to saw"

"So this is Spinalonga
a fortress protected from all foe
but who would want to live here
amidst a leper's woe"

I seemed to go and come from sleep
hardly with a pause
for a leper asleep can hardly weep
these are leper laws
and this painful hell I knew so well
had closed so many doors

In pain I'd held so many trials
though I could not apportion guilt
a month or a year had the same fear
as I felt my life melt
but I fought so hard to keep that life
and from this strength I built

In a month the doctor had told papa
that rather than keep me longer
he must sign the papers
and I must go to Spinalonga
an Island colony for lepers
where with others I'd be stronger

Papa begged at the doctor's knees
that I be spared the journey
the doctor coughed and held out a hand
but father had no money
and Stella led my father to bed
for he was so melancholy

Stella pledged that she would help
and flattered the doctor's dexterity
She thought me asleep so her secret would keep
as she swore her family affinity
and in the hall against the wall
she gave of her virginity

Spinalonga.

That I should give my life to thee
crumpled stone on crumpled knee
crumpled yet we both shall be
holding hands with the sea.

My aching head was a bundle of lead
and I could hardly see
so high a price for a brother's life
a sisters virginity
a bill to pay on judgement day
and my sister has twice the fee

I seemed to lie for so many months
whilst papa trod those stairs
and sister came quite often too
and spoke of her affairs
though she never mentioned the doctor
but I saw it in her stares

She never mentioned that noble deed
but I saw it in her eye
She'd given to secure the family ring
given because of I
a gauntlet of red her maidenhead
given to the lowest of high

I turned and tried to find a word
but words were hard to find
for my jaw was weak and I could not speak
but Stella was so kind
my eyes filled up as fast as a cup
and Stella squeezed my hand

Stella gripped and watched my face
and I managed the curve of a smile
but I turned to miss as she offered a kiss
and she knew she must leave me awhile
for the journey of sleep was travelling deep
and I'd already travelled a mile

In humid heat or a rain swept Crete
we saw the changing weather

It was papa's sixtieth birthday
a bracelet was placed on his arm
a drink or two of the Island brew
would do him little harm
When he offered a sip to a broken lip
I felt so very warm

I felt so very very warm
whilst papa was so merry
Stella sang a birthday song
and we ate a feast of curry
but there were signs between the lines
and for Stella I began to worry

It was several days later
when I found the opportunity to ask
Stella seemed so fidgety
unscrewing the lid of a flask
the tea was cold but I could not scold
when Stella completed the task

"What is the matter Stella
what thoughts are in your head
you can tell a brother
an invalid in bed"
my beautiful girl tried to smile
but her cheeks just flushed with red

"I have met a man and I am in love
to a marriage I would say yes
but to leave my papa would seem so far
from wearing a wedding dress
I sadly fear my brother dear
my life is in a mess"

a summers day faded away
in one square yard below us

I looked to Stella's saphire eyes
and felt the smile come to my face
I had a vision of Stella
in a gown of silk and lace
papa sat with a wedding hat
and a grin upon his face

I called for papa and he came at once
I gave him no time to speak
"Stella is to marry" I said
"to marry within a week
and you must approve with all your love
or my dying breath you'll take"

So papa gave his blessing
as they both sat on my bed
and we all shed tears for the many years
together we had had
and I felt the pain shoot down my arm
a stinging, burning red

I could not go to the wedding
for fear that I would be seen
but I heard the words the parson said
though sleep came in between
and a curious knell sounded in that bell
as I awoke from dream

When Stella had gone we managed a time
though I knew it wore his heart
a month had gone and the time had come
the time for us to part
I would go to the leper colony
and make a brand new start

The graveyard.

Tear stained stones, a final bed
teardrops that an ocean might have fed
to wash away what words were said
such perished youth, untimely dead.

I tossed my head in a heap of a bed
but sleeping was in vain
a dozen times in the humid heat
I must have called his name
my dear papa so near so far
at last my father came

"Hold my hand dear papa
I have so much I want to say
I've taken so much love from you
and now must go away
I cannot see you suffer for me
I'm leaving papa today"

He squeezed my hand and quietly said
"I've seen you grow so strong
but now it has the better of us
it seems to last so long
and I feel such a failure
for I have done so wrong."

"Shame not thyself lest thou become
as pessimistic as thy son
blame not thyself for deeds are done
blame not thyself for being wrong
for thou art close to heaven's own
and heaven is for the strong

For thou made light when it was dark
and warm when it was cold
and watched thy son by darkness sleep
and with each dawn unfold
and tended two needy babes
with a heart of burning gold

the journey of sleep was travelling deep
and I'd already travelled a mile

and truly father I say to thee
that which I see in thine eyes
is not guilt but tenderness
for thou hast nought to despise
so wipe away that tear papa
and clear those brilliant eyes

for when I go away from thee
I shall shed so many tears
but you must not pine for me papa
and you must have no fears
for God will watch for me thy son
and guide me through the years

"Hold me one more time my son
whilst this breath so shallow lingers
and keep those wounds covered son
for the sun so badly singes
and spreads with alarm this damning germ
that has robbed you of your fingers

the night has come and darkness falls
over the sea and over the sky
I see my shadow on the walls
of the boat in which I lie
my father and my sister
waving me goodbye

Such an angry sky and cruel sea
force the shadows to move
across the bed in which I sleep
upon the land I dearly love
and sparks fly in the sky
an angry Thor above

How gently sleeps my little boy
a million miles away in dream

So this is Spinalonga
a fortress protected from all foe
but who would want to live here
amidst a leper's woe
such a strange paradox
a paralysing blow!

My heart tells me that I should
try and learn to pray
for I'm sure that with God's help
I could find a way
to make my life more tolerable
in pieces of the day

Today I helped to build a house
though sadly it fell down
and at the end of it we all smiled
for in our work we had found
a spirit of togetherness
something quite profound

I have to go for water
it's such an awesome task
like climbing up a mountain
to fill a tiny flask
then the girls take it from me
but so nicely they always ask

Such an unhealthy Island
I've been on but two days
I've found somewhere to sleep
and watched the other lepers' ways
slowly heaping brick on brick
working with the clays

Remains of Michael Scarp.

Fortress surrounded by the deep
get thee from this ageless sleep
but whatever secrets hath thee keep
for this thirsty soil no more shall weep.

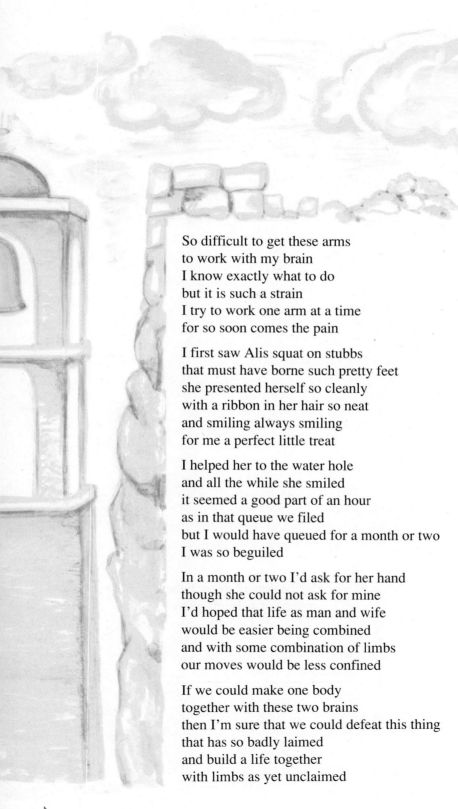

So difficult to get these arms
to work with my brain
I know exactly what to do
but it is such a strain
I try to work one arm at a time
for so soon comes the pain

I first saw Alis squat on stubbs
that must have borne such pretty feet
she presented herself so cleanly
with a ribbon in her hair so neat
and smiling always smiling
for me a perfect little treat

I helped her to the water hole
and all the while she smiled
it seemed a good part of an hour
as in that queue we filed
but I would have queued for a month or two
I was so beguiled

In a month or two I'd ask for her hand
though she could not ask for mine
I'd hoped that life as man and wife
would be easier being combined
and with some combination of limbs
our moves would be less confined

If we could make one body
together with these two brains
then I'm sure that we could defeat this thing
that has so badly laimed
and build a life together
with limbs as yet unclaimed

Its the duty of every father
to protect a sleeping son

Alis please say you will
for in my mind I crave
a longing for your pretty smile
so you can slay or save
put your pretty hand in mine
or your stubbled feet upon my grave

You will, you will Oh joyous bells
that ring so loudly in my ears
Alis, girl of my dreams
watch these unashamed tears
for the love that binds us together
will last for many, many years

If you could stand the pain Alis
could God bless us with a son
a son to forgive us every sin
with a mind to disgrace the moon
a son to bind us together for ever
a son to be with us soon

Oh my darling Alis
softer art thou than a sigh
sweeter than the fair Ophelia
whom at Hamlet's feet did lie
how proud I'd be for a son with thee
a son before I die

Alis gave a smile upon smile
though I knew that she was tired
even in pain there was never a drain
on the enthusiasm we'd fired
and she gave with great selflessness
as we tried to conceive that child

Path to the church.

Each time for one more day we pray
our timeless life in disarray
that man would every pray to die
on such a beautiful day.

In humid heat or a rain swept Crete
we saw the changing weather
it took a year and many a tear
we thought it would go on for ever
after some deception a sweet conception
We achieved together

My son is born to us this day
this is the happiest day of my life
Alis we have our own boy
courtesy of the surgeon's knife
Oh father do you see this
I have a son and a wife

I have drawn for us a circle
for our family a ring
to keep us close together
and protect us from within
our bonding will be binding
and will free us from all sin

We must call him Roberto, Alis
it is my father's name
to have such an equal chap
would make him quite profane
He will be so immensely proud
Roberto will have his brain

Two years old and how sturdy you look
my own little boy
soon you will do so many things
you are so sweet and coy
God's love from heaven above
and mummy's pride and joy

At the point of a knife I shall take this life
in this circle surrounded by sea

Come Alis quickly
come and look at this
our own boy Roberto
has caught for us a fish
We'll cook it for our dinner
it will make such a handsome dish

Today I have lit five candles
on a cake of milk and bread
and mummy's collected honey
and on your fingers spread
There's a present from the mainland
a garland for your head

How gently sleeps my little boy
a million miles away in dream
such a perfect little form
and it would seem
so sensitive to my aching arm
for his touch makes me beam

So sensitive to my aching arm
he grips transmitting comfort there
he beams with the moonbeams
he hasn't got a care
thumb firmly entrenched in a rainbow smile
he purrs away the midnight air

A letter from my sister
read it Alis, what does it say
"Sadly my dear brother
our father has passed away
and with his dying breath
these words he had to say

A ghostlike street.

This street that God hides from the sun
protected many an innocent one
listen for they are not gone
their ghosts forever linger on.

I'm happy you are married son
and have a circle of your own
but I wish that I could hold your hand
I feel so quite alone
I know that Stella will understand
a fathers love for a son

and life that is so unfair
to rob me of that son
fights with me for a final breath
to enter in my lung
I shed no tear for I fear
my circle is finally undone"

When father died dear brother
he held my hand to his face
I felt the dryness of his skin
there was no tear to trace
father died with some pride
his life he did not waste

Oh Alis, he was so proud a man
all those years of torment and strife
all those years for my sister and I
and so many without a wife
he worked so terribly, terribly hard
for such a modest life

Alis came and held my hand
I knew from her eyes she had something to say
but she would not add to my grief
it would keep for another day
but when that day finally came
she took my breath away

The first house.

Pretty window that has fed
these eyes from such a lonely bed
and brought such joy to this old head
of beauty were I free to tread.

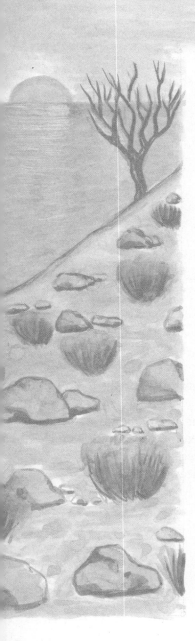

We were in the Church on Sunday
she asked me to help her pray
the tears streaked down her face
I could not hear what she tried to say
She mumbled all in broken words
"they'll take our boy away"

I put my arm around her
and tried to pull her near
"why will they take the boy" I said
"what is it that you fear
our boy is happy on the Island
why can't we keep him here?"

"I have learned a sad thing" she said
"I barely understand
for if our son is not a leper
he will be taken to the mainland
and fostered far away from us
away from our family band"

Almighty God who guides the world
help us in our prayer
for we cannot find a place to hide
the Island is too bare
I'd rather dwell in a dungeon cell
than see him go from here

There is an alternative Alis
to the dilemma we face today
an unkindly cut in the boy's foot
will do it I dare say
and we really have no choice Alis
or they'll take our boy away

House with fourteen steps leading to the roof.

fourteen steps to the door
I would there were eleven
for I swear that these three steps more
might be three steps to heaven.

Oh Alis, do not shun me
not shy away, not you
for you know that the boy we love
must be a leper too
that he should have a leper's blood
you know must be true

"I will not do it," Alis said
I cannot cut short so fair a life
please do not push me
take away the knife
please do not ask, such a task
it is not the duty of a wife

But Alis you must help me
they'll take away our happiness
the ring that binds us together
will fracture in distress
you promised love, by God above
your love is to the test

My son is now a leper
and I shall have him by my side
this cut and exchange of leper blood
shall his future guide
and here on this Island
he shall with us abide

These two days Roberto
and still she does not return
I know that she is unhappy
but of women I have much to learn
She's gone away, without a word to say
and I know in her head she has pain

77

The Archway

Stand, stay for just a moment
hidden from the glare
feel the hideous strife and torment
that ever lingers hear.

A messenger brings to me a note
a note as long as this
written with such an unsteady hand
with but a single kiss
"What have you done my Alis
What is it, what's amis!"

"My pain distresses me" she writes
but I could live the life we've built
but for the one unkindly cut
that gives me so much guilt
and flags my life unpurpose like
that I begin to wilt

That I can hardly hold the pen
that writes the words that swill in my head
I wish I could have told you
for these last moments I dread
goodbye my son and you sweet one
for I am untimely dead"

She has left us Roberto
left our leper race
for the deed your mother did for me
in life she could not face
The molten sting of our family ring
is such an evil place

They found her body yesterday
washed upon the sand
no pretty smile upon her face
no pretty ribbon band
but they said she grasped a piece of bark
so tightly in her hand

The gateway to the fortress.

Gateway to a fortress
more gateway to distress
less gateway to a fortress
for leper more or less

On the bark was written but one word
the name of you my son
even in her cold despair
she thought of you sweet one
and carved your mark on a piece of bark
and held it even when she'd gone

Oh Alis, what have I done
to one with so much life to live
to rob my son of half that life
I could not face the alternative
God forgive my selfishness
Oh Alis, can you forgive

Hold my hand Roberto
for I have life and yet
your mother's pain will scar my brain
and it will never let
me release a moments peace
until I've discharged this debt

Today we laid her down to rest
Roberto found some pretty flowers
and made such pretty patterns
we sat by the grave for hours
and a summers day faded away
in one square yard below us

Go to sleep my baby
please try not to cry
lay your head on mummy's pillow
by your daddy's side
and soon will come the morning
though I cannot think why

85

The second house.

Built by those who came
using every limb
a house of leper pain
with leper pain within.

Last night I wrote to Stella
and told her of my grief
I did not mention Roberto
my words were very brief
but I wrote that I was a taker of life
"Stella I am a thief"

Another day, another year
what track need I of time
for every day shows to me
the evil of my crime
my son is still and becomes more ill
and soon will run out of time

How pale you look my little boy
your legs have started to waste
and I see a twinge of sadness
such a sad little face
your mother bled, for the germ thats bred
for the germ that binds our race

Another letter from Basil
he always seems so jolly
in contrast to a brother of blood
who is so melancholy
A hospital in Crete has cured his feet
and he is to make a journey

"Basil is coming to see us Roberto
is that not good news
and you shall have a suit of clothes
anything you choose
We'll meet him at the shower pit
and take him to our house

89

The fallen house next to the quarry.

Houses never built to last
for leper perished in the past
had but a few bricks to cast
had but a few years to waste.

You and I shall prepare a feast
a feast of food and wine
and with my old friend Basil
we'll sit down to dine
we'll take a sip, a nostalgic trip
after such a long time

"My old friend Basil
what a wonderful suprise
when I read your letter
I could not believe my eyes
I am assured you're all but cured
but tell me make me wise."

"Well my good friend" he paused
to try and get his breath
"that first day that you found me
I was close to death
but a friend in need found a friend indeed
and now I am in health

I took a trip to Athens
and by a stroke of luck
I met a student doctor
who was noting in a book
different types of leprosy
and an interest in me he took

I soon became his patient
and he worked throughout the night
with different types of medicine
until he had a cure in sight
and out of the blue I suddenly knew
that he had got it right

93

The flats.

Flats in shade of cream or blue
reflect the sun or painful hue
for cry or tint describe the mew
of leprosy, in leper's view.

It was almost as if my raw wounds
changed a different shade of red
and in the night my pale white
grew a tinge of pink instead
He took his degree to Crete for me
and found a hospital bed

the rest is history, my friend
but the debt I owe is due
and I have saved for many years
and have brought this money to you
You have endured but will soon be cured
and Roberto too

Oh Basil can this really work
after all these years
the pain and the suffering
and Oh so many tears
that such joy for my own boy
could have fallen on Alis's ears

We did not go the next morning
for a tragedy occured
my son had died during sleep
it seems to me so obsurd
but the evenings wine had dulled my brain
and I had not heard a word

It seemed to take so many hours
to register in my head
the joyous rhyme of the evening time
turned disjointed prose instead
a boy dead in his mother's bed
and in my heart I hurt

The fallen house with overgrown garden.

As time and life are cast in stone
the garden flourishes, overgrown
reaching out on its own
as each of us, all alone.

In my heart and in every limb
I felt that cutting pain
I should have awoke, not let him choke
I felt such heavy blame
and the sullen knell of a church bell
would remind me of my shame

Death is such a final thing
that takes many an innocent one
but to creep in a mortal's sleep
leaves me quite undone
for it's the duty of every father
to protect a sleeping son

I laid him with his mother
and said my final prayers
God had let me pay my debt
and the interest was my tears
flowers of blue for the two
I left in neat layers

and now my story is over
as life will be over for me
I leave with God this suicide note
for I doubt with him I shall be
at the point of a knife I shall take this life
in this circle surrounded by sea

for my family I drew a circle
that should have lasted years
Roberto my son, Alis sweet one
my end so sadly nears
this circle of grief is a taker of life
on an Island so full of tears

101

The disinfection room.

Those who left the afflicted frame
showered here, away the pain
Brothers and sisters saw us lame
and many never came again.

An artist is to a poet
as poetry is to art

to my friend Stephen Driver of Wakefield
for his paintings.